D1376345

Tópé Arrives

Wendy Hue

Illustrated by Zara Slattery

authorHOUSE®

AuthorHouse™ UK Ltd.
500 Avebury Boulevard
Central Milton Keynes, MK9 2BE
www.authorhouse.co.uk
Phone: 08001974150

This book is a work of fiction. People, places, events, and situations are the product of the author's imagination. Any resemblance to actual persons, living or dead, or historical events, is purely coincidental.

First published by AuthorHouse 04/08/2011

ISBN: 978-1-4567-7640-4

Edited by Laura Atkins, Children's Literature Specialist

For my family and friends. W.H.

I would like to thank my editor, Laura Atkins, my illustrator, Zara Slattery and also the Hilary Johnson Authors' Advisory Service for the help and support that they have given during the writing of this book.

CONTENTS

Nigeria   1

England   12

School in a new land   21

Tears   31

Football Tournament   38

Special Things   47

Sleepover   59

Star Youth Academy   70

The Dundun Drummers   80

Nigeria

The smells in my house have changed, and Aunty Yemmy doesn't cook jollof rice like Mum. Hers is too peppery for me and Mum's was golden. I wrinkle my nose at the sharp, stale smell of Uncle Olu's aftershave.

I can't sleep, so I wake up before anyone else and stand at the front door looking out at the dawn sky, listening to the sounds of Ibadan as the town comes to life. A red truck with oranges and tomatoes on the back is heading for Dugbe Market. Everything has changed since the car crash. Aunty Yemmy and Uncle Olu have come over from England and are staying in my house. They say they are going to take me back with them the day after tomorrow, but I'm not so sure. Nigeria is my home.

Slowly, I creep to my parents' bedroom. I turn the cold door handle and look inside. The big bed is neat and no one has slept in it, but I can still smell them. Tears run down my face, and I'm surprised; it's the first time I've cried since everything changed.

I never cry. I didn't cry at the funeral; I just stood and stared. Everyone has been saying kind words and lots of people keep hugging me, but it's like a horrible dream.

I stand at the bedroom door. Huge heaving sobs take my breath. Aunty Yemmy finds me here. She says nothing but holds me tight and strokes my back.

The rest of the morning goes by in a blur and I sit in the front room glancing at the headlines on the front pages of the newspapers, which are sitting on the small glass table near me.

'Fatal Road Crash on Route to Village.'

'University Lecturer's Boy Made Orphan in Road Crash out of Ibadan.'

In the afternoon, John, Edwin and Abi come to the front door. They stand there grinning, just the same as always. Abi has found my football and he's doing tricks with it, sliding it behind his back and bouncing it off his head and knee.

'Coming out to play, Tópé?' asks Abi.

I hesitate, and then look at Aunty Yemmy. She smiles, the first time I have seen her smile properly since she came here over a week ago.

'Go along, Tópé,' she says. 'Go and have fun.'

She gives us each a little bag of chin chin and stands at the door, her arms folded. Though her mouth is smiling, her eyes are red and swollen as if she's been crying. Then, just as we are leaving, she calls after me. 'Don't be late, Tópé. We have to pack up because we leave tomorrow morning.'

The words hit me like thunder. I can't help but glare at Aunty.

'Yes, your suitcase must be zipped up... tonight,' Aunty continues in a soft voice.

I walk outside to the veranda and look down at the dry tiled floor. My body trembles and I can't pretend any more.

As we approach the play area Abi passes the ball to me.

'Can someone else be goalie today?' I ask, dribbling the ball at my feet.

'Sure,' says John.

Then I kick the ball hard towards John and he curls it near me. I kick it once again, even harder this time, until the dust flies from the ground.

'Okay, okay,' says Edwin. 'Calm down, Tópé. We're not even there yet.'

I look to the big, towering gate of the compound. Abi passes the ball to me as we reach the football area and I run along kicking it so fiercely that now there are clouds of orange dust everywhere.

'Are you annoyed with us, Tópé?' Edwin asks as he takes the ball.

4

'No,' I say. Then I wrestle the ball back and kick it wicked and fast again, until it disappears between the light green and blue houses in the compound, over the high white flaky wall.

'Look what you've done now,' says John.

'What?' I say.

'You've kicked the ball out of the compound,' says Abi. 'Didn't you see?'

'I'll get it,' I say.

As I race to the big, open, metal gates of the compound I can hear my friends calling, but I keep going. Their voices disappear as I run, with my dry feet just touching the hot ground and sweat dripping from my head. Car horns are honking, and all I can see is a foggy blaze of colour. Street sellers are everywhere; some with baskets on their heads, some frying yellow plantain, some roasting yam. I'm going so fast, I accidentally knock over an old lady's red and green chilli peppers. I shout, 'Sorry! Sorry Aunty!'

Then I see my ball sitting on the floor near some tinned tomatoes, so I swoop it up, clutch it under my arm and continue to run. I hear Abi shouting behind me, 'Tópé! Tópé! Stop!' And I look back to see him running after me. I run faster and faster away from the busy area, clambering up a slope where there are goats grazing. My eyes zoom all over the place, and then I fall to the ground, gasping for breath. I bury my head in the dry grass and start to sob.

Abi has caught up with me and bends down near my face on the ground. Our eyes meet and he says, 'Tópé, what's wrong?'

I shiver then say, 'I don't want to go without my mum and dad. If they didn't die then I wouldn't have to leave. I wish they could come back and I want to stay in Nigeria.'

'Yes, but England is great, too. Plus, my mum has told me that we are going on holiday there next year,' says Abi.

'Everyone else might want to go, but not me. And my dad told me that England was a cold place.'

'It's not always cold, Tópé. England has all different kinds of weather – my mum has told me.'

At that moment, I make my decision and say, 'I'm not going to England, Abi.' Then we both go quiet for a moment and all I can hear is one of the bells on the goats jingling. I feel so hot and my mind spins, but then I close my wet eyes for a minute. I tilt my head. 'Abi, listen. I think that is Uncle I can hear calling my name.' I quickly look around and notice a tiny little wooden hut with a wavy roof up the slope. 'Let's stay in there and hide so he can't find me. Then I can stay in Nigeria and won't have to leave,' I say.

'Okay,' says Abi.

We squash together inside the dark hut, but in no time at all Uncle's head appears in the doorway and he gasps, 'So there you are.' He's out of breath and pauses before continuing. 'I was so worried about you when you ran off. And then I saw Abi racing after you. Can I join the two of you?'

'Yes, okay,' Abi replies.

Uncle squashes in beside us. 'Are you two okay?' he asks.

I sniffle.

Uncle looks me right in the eye and puts one hand on my left shoulder. 'Everything will be fine, Tópé. I know it will take a very long time to get over this – and that's if we ever do. I, too, cannot believe I've lost my only brother-in-law and your aunty her only brother. But Aunty and I will look after you. We will never replace your parents, but we will love you as our own. Your cousins, Femi and Happy, are so looking forward to you coming. Happy kept jumping up and down saying your name over and over before we left.'

At this point Abi says, 'And don't forget I'm coming to see you next year, Tópé.' He looks thoughtful for a moment then says, 'I don't know who I will sit next to in class now, though.'

Then Uncle says, 'Tópé, I'm sorry we could not stay in Nigeria a little longer so that you could say goodbye to everyone properly. But I have to get back to my job in England by Monday because my company is very strict.'

No words can help me right now, so I just sit quietly.

Eventually, Uncle and Abi stop talking and I look up and beyond my sore eyes. Uncle's foot accidentally touches my football and I notice it rolling away down the slope. I get up fast and chase after it, and then hold it to my body.

'Come!' Uncle calls to me from the hut, as he struggles to stand up in the cramped space and squeezes his body through the opening. 'Look at the goats; they know it's going to rain soon.'

I say nothing and just watch the goats shuffling under the tree before I begin to walk slowly with

Abi beside and Uncle in front of me. Rain begins to fall, and just as we are reaching the gates to our compound the lights suddenly blink out.

'A power cut,' says Uncle. 'Look, the lights from the hair salon have gone out.' Everything is dark and quiet.

'My dad is not here to wind up the generator,' I say as we reach the white wall of the compound shimmering in the dark.

'I will do that. You go inside the house while I take Abi home to the house next door but one, as it's getting late. I will be there in a minute. See you in a short while, Tópé,' he says as he and Abi walk towards Abi's home.

'See you in the morning, Tópé,' calls Abi in the pouring rain. I don't want tomorrow morning to come so I don't reply and just watch their shadows rushing in the dark.

There's no sign of Aunty as I feel my way around the shadowy house with only flickers of light coming in through the windows from the full moon. I head for my room in the blackness, feeling the walls with my arms stretched out, throw my football down, plonk myself on my bed and start to bite my nails. I close my eyes, rub my face with my hands, then look down at my football. The moon outside my window is shining on it. Then I hear a car horn hooting and I think of the crash again – and my mum and dad – then my mind goes blank. Suddenly, with a mind of its own, my body stands up firm and my left foot kicks the ball at my bedroom wall. It bounces back at me hard and hits my left shoulder. Then I kick and kick again, until a wall gecko darts off. My ball keeps bouncing back at me, and the more I do it the harder I kick it with all of my strength. Then I give it one vicious kick and it smashes into the wooden carved boat my mum gave me. I can hear some of the tiny wooden people from the boat splatter over my room like bullets, and the small bodies shoot like sparks in the shadows.

I run out of my room with my fists clenched and dash out through the front door. Rain hits me hard as I reach the back of the house and start punching the wall. My knuckles begin to bleed, and I stand crying into the rough wall. I hear Aunty calling behind me.

'Oh Tópé,' she says and cuddles me in the rain. 'Come, let's go indoors.' And she puts her arm around my shoulder and leads me back. We are soaked and water drips from my head and the bottom of Aunty's blue dress. She cleans my sore hands and puts a plaster on each knuckle, then says, 'Tópé, go and change out of your wet clothes before we talk.'

I notice the electricity goes back on as I enter my room because lights from nearby houses shine through and make my eyelids flicker, so I turn on my bedroom light. I see one of the people from the wooden boat sitting on the floor in the corner. I kneel down and scramble about on the floor to find the rest of the people to put them back in their seats, but the three people that sat at the front – who my dad said reminded him of me, him and Mum – are missing. I look under my bed, on the floor, on my bed, but they are nowhere to be seen.

I sit on my bed and then Uncle and Aunty come in my room and sit either side of me. They begin talking in kind voices about me going to England and Uncle having to get back to the mail company he works for, but I don't want to listen, so I just sit and wait from them to finish. Eventually, Uncle gets up and says, 'It's getting very late and we must be up early.' Then he smiles at me and I smile back, but I don't feel any better.

'Now, here is your case, Tópé,' Aunty says, pulling a brown suitcase from under my bed. 'You need to choose what you want to bring and fit it all in here.'

'Aunty, my football has to go in,' I say. 'And my boat too.'

'Let's give your football a wipe over,' Aunty says as she takes my ball, 'then I'm sure we can find some space to fit it in, even if I have to sit on the case to zip it up. But your boat will get destroyed in the case, Tópé. It's probably best to leave it here.'

'But, I have to take the boat, too.'

'Well, it's either the boat or the ball, Tópé. Both won't fit in.'

'Urm! Urm...!' I mumble.

'I think you are tired with all that urming you are mumbling, Tópé,' says Aunty.

'But, but, my boat...' I come out with.

'No buts, Tópé. We really must get packed up. I think you are more football crazy than boat crazy – the ball it is,' answers Aunty as she begins stuffing my clothes in the case.

I really do not want my boat left behind. I always liked my boat but now it is more precious then ever.

'There we are, Tópé,' says Aunty, as she fits my ball in and struggles to close my suitcase. 'Now I must find a bright ribbon to tie around the handle so that we recognise it when we get off the aeroplane.'

'What about this football sticker, Aunty?' I ask and hand her one of the treasured stickers that Abi gave me. At least I'll have something that Abi gave me coming with me.

'Perfect,' she says and slaps the sticker on the side of the case. 'Now, we must sleep. It's late and we have to rise early. Goodnight, Tópé. See you in the morning,' Aunty says as she turns off the light and shuts the door.

I feel more tired than ever before. I think about my ball in the case. Right now, this is all I want to think about, but I do wonder about my boat as I focus on its outline in the dark. My bulging case is sitting near the chair and my eyes begin to focus in on my football sticker. I'm sleepy, but I can't get to sleep and toss and turn in my bed. I start to count sheep in my head, as that's what Mum said I should do whenever I couldn't sleep. Dad said count the shadows or the cricket chirps. I don't feel like counting shadows tonight, so I listen to the chirps and count those instead.

Finally, my eyes begin to close.

England

I wake up, get out of bed and stretch my arms. I can hear people talking in my house.

'Hi, Tópé. We've come to say goodbye,' Abi says as he puts his head around my bedroom door. John and Edwin are right behind him smiling. John comes in and picks up my wooden boat. He says, 'I suppose you won't need this any more, Tópé, now that you are going to England.'

I say, 'Put it down, John. It's mine and no one is having my boat – ever.'

John gently puts my boat down on the table and says, 'Cool it, Tópé – it's a little wooden boat.'

'I wish I could go to England,' says Edwin.

I sigh.

'Come on, Tópé, let's start moving,' says Aunty as she jostles between my friends. 'You boys can come and help us put the luggage into the car while Tópé dresses and has some breakfast,' she says, and my friends follow her. Aunty finishes with, 'and Tope, I have a nice warm jacket here I brought from England for you to put on when we get there, but I'll hold on to it for you for now.' I look at this black mass of a monster jacket, which I cannot imagine putting around my body.

Slowly, I get dressed.

As I walk out of my bedroom with my hand luggage strapped over my shoulder, I turn and look at my wooden boat sitting isolated, with me and my mum and dad missing. Then I walk to my mum and dad's room, open the door and stand at the entrance looking in. The room is still and quiet. I close my mouth and eyes and breathe in slowly, but heavily. I think of my mum and dad smiling and lying in bed, the way they did on Saturdays until I came in to wake them up and say good morning. Then the moment is gone and I can hear everyone outside saying, 'Where is Tópé? Where is Tópé?' A couple of tears drop down my cheeks. I leave, but turn around and take one last look at my home. Suddenly, I dash back to my room, pull my hand luggage bag from my shoulder, dig out the writing book and pencil and the reel of football stickers then gently place my wooden boat inside. It's too long to fit in properly, so a little bit of the boat peeps out to one side. As I head outside, Edwin and Abi are struggling with my suitcase, and John is standing by the car writing his name on one of the dusty glass windows. The sun is shining on my cream and red house and the cashew tree nearby is full. I step outside.

So many people who live in our compound have got up early to say goodbye. I put my hand up and wave from the back seat as my dad's best friend, Emmanuel, drives us to Murtala Muhammed International Airport in Ikeja. Aunty Lola, the old lady in the house next door, is waving from her veranda, with her walking stick in her other hand. And I can see my friends making funny faces and waving to me as we start to drive away. Abi shouts out, 'See you next year,' and then he starts running with his arms wide out, pretending he's an aeroplane. I watch him become smaller in the distance. I feel so sick, but at the same time he makes me laugh.

The airport is so busy and hot with lots of people dragging big suitcases and chatting and laughing and arguing. My mind is in a whirl as we board a massive plane. I sit in the middle, between Aunty and Uncle, and my ears pop when the aeroplane takes off so I put my hands over them. I look at the clouds out of a tiny window and say goodbye to Nigeria. I still don't want to leave. What will England be like? I hope I meet someone who knows my dad and went to Greenwich University like he did. Then I can talk about my dad. I lean on Aunty and soon doze off.

My eyes begin to open when I hear an announcement saying, 'We will shortly be arriving. Please fasten your seatbelts.' The aeroplane bumps a bit and everyone on the aeroplane claps when it stops. I don't clap.

I feel squashed as everyone stands up at the same time to get their hand luggage from the shelves.

'What is that sticking out of your bag, Tópé?' asks Aunty as everyone shuffles about and she passes it to me. I don't respond.

As I get off the aeroplane, Aunty gives me the enormous thick jacket and says, 'Here, Tópé. Put this on to keep you warm.' She looks serious, so I pull on this heavy jacket and it makes me feel horrible. I feel as if I'm stifling.

I look back at the huge aeroplane with wings on both sides. I feel like an aeroplane with both of my wings missing. I shiver and my ears and nose are so cold.

We wait with lots of people before our suitcases arrive. Most people here don't look like my friends and others in Ibadan. Most are the same pale colour as the family that came to visit our church. Aunty and Uncle's suitcases come, but not mine. Then I spot mine, too. It is coming round on this moving thing like a racetrack for cars, so I say to Aunty and Uncle, 'There it is: the one with the football sticker on it.'

'Good spotting, Tópé,' says Uncle.

'Let's go and find the car now, Tópé. We'll get a courtesy bus to the car park.' I don't know what this is, but follow.

I slide the black monster jacket on. It feels horrible. Then we board a bus with lots of people with suitcases. We get off at a stop that says 2B and begin looking for the car. I've never seen so many cars together before, hundreds and hundreds. I take the heavy jacket off again because walking is making me hot. I don't like wearing jackets because they feel heavy and I don't usually wear them in Nigeria.

'Ah! There it is,' calls Uncle, pointing to a silver bus-looking car. 'Now we can head home to Peckham.'

'But I thought we were going to London?' I say.

'Yes we are, Tópé,' says Aunty. 'Peckham is a part of London – a very vibrant place, full of colour.'

Once Uncle and Aunty put our cases in the back, we start driving away from the enormous car park. I sit in the back on my own, biting my fingernails and looking out at this very strange place. First, we zoom along a big, smooth grey road and soon I see lots of enormous green and brown fields and then I see a red tractor. My granddad had a tractor in the village in Nigeria, but his was green. I then see lots of little houses that are all touching sides with each other and some have a little chimney on top. The houses are made of lots and lots of tiny rectangle bricks stuck together. I don't see so many of these in Nigeria. It must have taken a long time to stick them together. I had imagined that the houses would be much bigger in England, and only a few of them have been painted. Lots of the doors are painted different colours though.

I see skyscrapers similar to ones I've seen in Ibadan. I like tall buildings because they nearly touch the sky.

'You okay, Tópé?' asks Aunty. 'You'll have no nails left if you carry on biting them,' she continues with a smile.

I stop biting my nails and nod yes.

After what seems like a very long drive, Uncle says, 'Here we are, Tópé. Look, there's Femi waving at the window.' I see a house that is the same colour as the dirt on the floor in the play area of my compound in Nigeria. A green bush is near the blue door.

As I step out of the car and walk towards the house, a short woman in a pink top, who I've never seen before, comes out and stands at the door. 'Hi everybody,' she calls out. She watches me as I walk up the pathway. 'You must be Tópé. Come inside the sitting-room,' she says, and leads me through a very narrow hallway with a big plant to the side and then into another room. 'I'm Aunty Ajoke –

Aunty Yemmy's sister. I've been looking after your cousins.' She hugs me and I smile.

Femi walks out and says, 'Hi Tópé.' I recognise him from when he came to visit us last year. At nine years old he's the same height as me, even though I'm a year older. I smile at him and he smiles back. As he goes to hug his parents, they tell him to welcome me. I notice that they mostly speak English and not Yoruba at home. Happy then runs up and grabs my legs and I grin, even though I nearly fall over and have to hold my hand luggage tight.

Everyone is laughing and joking, but I just stand back and watch. I look in the corner of the sitting-room and see three Dundun Drums, which make me think of home. My granddad in Nigeria could play all of those drums really well and sometimes he showed my dad and me how to play them when we went to visit him, even though I found it was too hard to learn. Right now I don't even want to touch them; what's the point? My dad is no longer with me and neither is Granddad.

Happy won't stop staring at me, but then she gives me a cheeky grin. And there is so much food on the big glass table that is in the adjoining room. Some of it I recognise, but some looks and smells so odd.

'Let me show you our bedroom, Tópé,' says Femi. 'Up here,' he points as I follow him up some steep stairs. I count twenty-five steps. My home in Nigeria only had six steps near the front door and they didn't have thick fabric on them.

Uncle brings my suitcase upstairs and the first thing I do is unzip it and take my football out.

'This is your bed, Tópé,' Uncle says, and points to the bed near the window. 'I'll leave you two for now.'

I place my football at the bottom of the bed that is for me, then I open my hand luggage and reach in to take out the wooden boat, but realise that most of the people are littered in the bottom of my bag. Maybe I didn't glue them properly when I was still in Nigeria. I pick them out of my bag and place them back in their seats. Femi helps me.

'I've got some glue. We could stick them back in place, but it looks like some are missing,' says Femi.

'Yes, I already know that three of the people are missing,' I say.

'Okay, well, I didn't know, and you can't put your football on the bed, Tópé. Mum won't let you do that,' Femi says.

I look at Femi hard then take my football and place it on the floor – for now, anyway, but at this moment I need to sort out my boat.

'Do you still want me to help you glue back the people you found in your bag?' asks Femi.

'No thanks. I'll do it myself now,' I reply.

'Okay then. Here's the glue.' Femi hands it to me and heads out of the room.

I sit looking around the light blue room, which has a football-patterned shade hanging from the ceiling and a rug on the floor that is like a football pitch. I glance at my boat and begin to glue the little people back to their seats safely. They are quite fiddly in my fingers, but I handle them as gently as possible.

All weekend I want to be sick, and I don't really listen when anyone speaks to me.

On Sunday evening, Femi and I go up to bed early and he sits playing a computer game. Aunty has been nagging me to finish unpacking, so I take out the last of my clothes from my suitcase. At the very bottom of the cracked leather bag I spot something. It's the smallest of the wooden people that is missing from my boat. It must have fallen in there when I kicked my ball in Nigeria.

'Femi, can I borrow your glue again, please?'

He ignores me.

'Femi,' I say louder, 'can I use your glue?'

'Yeah, do what you want. I'm busy, my birthday is next week and I'm doing a list of who can come. It's over there on the floor,' he points.

'Thanks,' I say.

I put the small wooden figure back in the boat where it belongs, make sure all of the other people are properly secured and look at the two empty seats. Why are Mum and Dad not here? Then I put my football back on the bottom of the bed.

On Sunday night, as I lie in my new bed wondering what my new school will be like in the morning, I look at my wooden boat on the side-table near to me with my mum and dad missing. Femi starts telling me all about the school and the teachers, the dinners and the after-school football club. He says he thinks that I will like my new school, but I'm not so sure.

Then Femi quietly says, 'Tópé, are you still awake?'

I turn on my side, looking at the wall in the dark and pretend to be asleep. I don't answer.

School in a new land

As our room starts to light up with the dim morning sun, I lie watching Femi with his eyes half-open, but he's fast asleep. Then I lift the see-through white curtain near to the window and peep through. The sun wants to come out, but the sky won't let it. I see a bird sitting on top of a grey building. It has a little red circle on its belly. There are so many tall buildings with glass windows and not as many houses like the one I'm in. The bird flies off. My mouth and tummy have a dizzy feeling again, so I get up and go down the hallway to the bathroom. I glance in the mirror and see my puffy eyes. I heave over the toilet, but nothing comes out.

I go back to bed and continue to watch Femi sleeping on the other side of the room. He's all right, apart from when he told me I couldn't put my football on the bed. And then I hear that weird clanking noise that I've heard coming from the radiator every morning since I've been here.

Happy puts her head around the door and makes a funny face at me. I smile at her, but she just stares back with the funny face. Then she bangs open the door and wakes Femi. He sits up and belts out, 'Happy, I've told you to knock before you come in my room. You are three now and should be able to do that at your age.' Then he rubs his eyes.

Happy runs off calling, 'Mama! Mama!'

'Come on, Tópé. We have to get ready for school,' says Femi putting his feet out of his bed. 'I'm going to use the bathroom first,' he tells me and dashes off. Little does he know that I've already been to the bathroom this morning.

I stay in bed and look at my uniform hanging up on the wardrobe door. My uniform in Nigeria was green and brown and here it is blue, and the trousers are long. My new shoes are still in the box, so I get up and take them out and have another good look at them. They are black and very special and shiny. I shove the box underneath my bed.

Femi is back in a flash and has water splashed all over his face. I go to the bathroom and look in the mirror again, but then turn away because my eyes look so droopy. I brush my teeth. My mouth is dry.

Femi and I get dressed, then he rushes downstairs. I slowly follow.

'Good morning, boys,' says Uncle as he enters the kitchen. 'Monday mornings are not always my best, but this Monday is special, Tópé, because you start your new school today.'

I take one mouthful of cereal, then try to take another, but just can't put the spoon to my mouth again.

'Are you okay, Tópé?' asks Uncle.

I nod yes, but feel horrible.

We all get in the car and drive to my new school. As I sit biting my fingernails, we go through many traffic lights. My stomach is still knotted up in the middle and my head thumps.

We reach the school gates and Femi says, 'There's my mate, Joe, over there waving his hand at me to come. See you at break time, Tópé.' Then he rushes over to a bunch of boys that are staring at me.

Uncle and Aunty take me into school with Happy. A tall white man with grey-silver, spiky hair and a pointed nose comes towards us. He says, 'Hi! Is this young *Too-Pee*? Lovely to meet you. I'm your new head teacher and my name is Mr Gordon.' He can't say my name. I look to the shiny wooden floor.

'It's Tópé, Mr Gordon; pronounced *Top-pay,*' says Uncle.

'I do apologise, Tópé,' Mr Gordon says.

I look up. He has light blue eyes, like the sky in Nigeria, and he blinks a lot. He smiles and puts his hand out to shake mine. His hand is warm. Then he says, 'Let me take you to your new class, Tópé.'

Uncle says, 'Goodbye, Tópé. Have a good day.' Then Aunty hugs me. I wish she wouldn't hug me so tight. Happy then grabs my legs and looks up at me with a smile. I nearly tumble over.

'Happy,' warns Aunty.

I wave goodbye.

Mr Gordon takes me down a long echoey corridor. On either side I can see lots of children looking at me from cramped, box-like classrooms with closed glass windows all the way down the hallway. In Nigeria, some of my classes were outside and the windows were nearly always open. Mr Gordon then leads me through a large door that says 6T and speaks to a short white woman with long yellow hair. The room is humming with lots of chatter and far more noise than my class in Nigeria. As I look across the room, I can see many eyes on me and one girl pointing my way.

'This is Tópé, Miss Turner, the new boy starting today.' He turns to me and says, 'I'm sure you'll be very happy here, but do come and speak to me if anything is bothering you.' He blinks his eyes a few more times, and then says, 'Enjoy your first day,' before he disappears.

'Come on, everyone, settle down now,' calls Miss Turner.

Miss Turner, she has big blue eyes and a tiny mouth. She has a smiley, wide face.

I look around the classroom and see so many books and pictures on the walls. Then I see the same blue dictionary I had in my class in Nigeria. I remember my friends in my class back home and smile.

Miss Turner turns to the class and says, 'I'd like you to welcome Tópé who has joined us.' Then she turns to two boys in the far right corner and says, 'Randall and Terry, I'd be grateful if you could look after Tópé. Please take him to the cloakroom and show him where he can hang his coat, and also where the toilets are. Join me on the Charles Dickens table when you get back.'

Randall is Asian-looking with straight black hair, and Terry is shorter with straight light creamy - coloured hair; he is wearing the best trainers I have ever seen.

When we return, Miss Turner calls out the names of the people in my class. There is a girl called Grace Adebola who looks like she's from home and she has the same hairstyle as John's little sister in Nigeria. The class is very noisy and everyone is messing about and giggling. In my class in Nigeria Mr Fashakin would have gotten angry, but Miss Turner just keeps calling the names louder and louder.

'Right class! Quiet down, please, and line up for us to go into assembly,' Miss Turner shouts.

We walk along the corridor and enter a huge room that has a stage with curtains. There are loads of people sitting on the floor in rows. We sit on chairs in my school in Nigeria and not the floor. My class go to the back of the big room.

Lots of kids stare at me and I can see two girls looking at me and whispering to each other. I wish I still had Abi in my class. He'd suggest something funny, like making silly faces at them.

After I sit down, I glimpse Femi three rows in front. He turns around and smiles. Then Mr Gordon comes on to the stage and begins to talk, but instead of paying attention, I look out of the window and watch the clouds moving. I glance in front of me and notice Femi's friend, Joe, looking at the clouds as well. I think of my mum and how she always wanted me to try hard at things to succeed, but this new life of mine is so hard.

After about an hour in assembly, we return to our class, and it is soon break time. Miss Turner claps three times at the class and says angrily, 'If you think I didn't notice paper aeroplanes being fired around the class whilst I was seeing to Samantha, then you are all mistaken. For that you will all go to break five minutes late.' Randall made the aeroplanes first and threw them, but Miss didn't see. She gives more chances than Mr Fashakin did, though, and I like that.

As we dash out into the playground, Femi comes over and asks if I want to play football with him and his mates. I say yes, even though I am unsure, as I don't know if they have different rules in England and I'm not used to playing here. However, after Femi passes the football to me and I start doing kick-ups on the spot, I realise that I play just as well here. Femi then introduces me to his friends. There is Joe, who has spiky hair, a pointed nose, little dots on his face and a pinched expression; Sebastian, who has wavy hair and a big smile; and Sean, who is thin and wears glasses. Randall and Terry from my class join in, too.

Two of Femi's friends, Joe and Sean, give me very strange looks as I continue to control the ball, and then Joe looks at me hard and says, 'Weirdo.' But no one else takes any notice as their eyes are on the ball.

I sprint near to Sean and tackle him, using my twisty foot tricks, until he gives up. Then Joe comes in on my right, trying to wrestle with me. I screen the ball to my left side then dribble clear and boot it right in to the goal – it hits the bottom corner and slips in with ease. Maybe I'm good at playing in England, too.

'Yeah! Wicked, Tópé!' shouts Sebastian.

Joe gives me a dirty look. Then the bell rings. I don't think he likes me much.

When we are back in class, Miss Turner tells us that we all have to pick a reading book from the library corner and put it in our reading pack folders for home time. I choose a book with a footballer on the front.

During lunchtime, I don't see Femi. It turns out that when my year is having dinner, his year is out playing. The dinner hall has a different smell from my old school, and I don't recognise any of the food, apart from the stinky chips.

By afternoon break, Randall, Terry and I meet up again with Femi, Sean, Sebastian and Joe. They are kicking a ball about.

'I'm not playing with him,' Joe says with his chin pointing out.

'Yeah, he's weird,' adds Sean.

'Doesn't matter,' says Sebastian, smiling at me. 'He's good at football.'

'He's a weirdo,' says Joe as he kicks the ball with force.

'Shut your mouth, Joe,' Femi spits. 'If you don't cut it out you're not coming to my party next week.'

'Don't care,' Joe shouts back.

I walk away. Terry follows me. He says, 'Just ignore them, Tópé.'

Femi comes running up behind us and says, 'Are you okay?'

Then a woman with long straight brown hair comes up to us and says, 'Is everything okay with you boys?'

Femi says, 'Yes, we're fine thanks, Miss Pearce.'

The bell goes and it's time to go back to our classrooms. Femi quickly says to me, 'She's one of the helpers,' before he goes to his classroom and Terry, Randall and I go to ours.

'It's "Golden Time" this afternoon, Tópé, and we can choose whatever we want to do until home time,' says Randall.

The words 'Golden Time' make me think of my mum, because of the yummy golden-looking jollof rice she cooked. Terry, Randall and I decide to do painting, but my mind wanders again. I look out of the window and up to the sky and think about my mum – the kind way she used to look at me, with her glowing cheeks and wide smile.

Soon the bell rings and it's time to go home.

When I come out of my classroom I see Aunty waving at me and Happy is standing next to her. I see Femi coming, too. As Aunty drives us home, Femi tells her about a letter he has about a school trip to a farm in Devon. I sit quietly in the back clutching on to my reading folder.

'How was your day today, boys?' Uncle asks as we walk through the door.

'Okay,' I reply.

'Joe was being horrible in the playground,' Femi says.

'What do you mean?' asks Aunty.

'He was saying Tópé was a weirdo,' Femi replies.

'Just ignore him, Tópé,' says Uncle.

'I'm not having that,' says Aunty. 'Do you want me to have a word with Miss Turner?'

'No, it's all right, Mum,' says Femi.

'And are these the same boys you have invited to your swimming party?' Aunty asks.

'Yes, they are,' Femi answers.

'Well, maybe you need to ask yourself if they really are your friends,' Aunty says.

'Tópé, do you want me to have a word?' Aunty asks.

'No, it's all right, Aunty. I will be okay,' I say, not wanting to make things worse. I feel so sick and my head hurts again like it did this morning.

'Well, so long as you are sure. But if it happens again I want to know. Will you promise me?' she asks.

'Yes, Aunty,' I reply.

'Anyway, it's time to eat. I've cooked some soup.'

Aunty has made a yummy egusi soup with pounded yam, but I can hardly eat what is in front of me. I force down some mouthfuls, but it's such an effort. In Nigeria, I would use my hands to eat this and gobble it up fast.

After dinner, Femi and I do some reading with Uncle in our room, and I get loads of words wrong. Ever since I have come here I find it hard to concentrate on my reading. In Nigeria Mr Fashakin used to say I was such a good reader and sometimes he asked me to read out loud to the class.

Uncle says, 'You must be tired, Tópé. Let's just chat for a while before bedtime.' Femi gets up to go to the loo. Uncle looks at my wooden boat and says, 'Your boat is well made, Tópé, even though two of the people are missing. Do you know I used to help your grandfather make wooded carved objects back home in Nigeria, and even drums when I was about your age? Those days in the village were very special to me.'

'My granddad and dad told me about the Dundun Drums,' I say. I manage to smile and wonder if I could perhaps make the little figures of my parents if I tried. But then I realise that I wouldn't even know where to start. Femi comes back in the bedroom and he and Uncle continue to chat, but I just nod and listen to them. I keep thinking about so many things that my head feels dizzy – my mum, my dad, Nigeria, my day at school today, everything – and I just hope tomorrow is better.

Tears

A whole week goes by and everything seems much the same. I'm looking forward to Femi's birthday party, though. I've never been to a party in England. Aunty drops Femi and me off before school starts and we go into the playground to kick my ball around a bit.

I see Joe and Sebastian entering the school gates. Femi calls over and says, 'Do you want to play with us?'

'I'm not playing with him,' says Joe, looking at me.

'Yeah,' says Sean. Then they both start chanting, 'Weirdo! Weirdo! Tópé is a weirdo!'

I bow my head because my eyes start watering. I blink to clear them and then give Joe and Sean an evil stare. Femi looks angry with them, too, and then he calls out, 'Right, that's it! You're not coming to my party tonight if you don't cut it.' He puts his arm around me and says, 'Don't listen to them, Tópé.'

Miss Pearce comes over and says, 'Are you two okay there? I hope you're settling in, Tópé.'

Tears roll down my cheeks. I want to stop them, but I can't.

'Come with me to the Rainbow Room, boys,' Miss Pearce says. She leads us to a blue and yellow room that has a poster on the wall that says, 'If you are feeling unwell at school this is the place to be.' It's small, but very colourful with rainbows and fluffy clouds painted on the walls. Femi and I sit on the bed. I'm too upset to say anything. Right now I so want my mum and dad. I don't think they know what they have done to me.

The head teacher walks by and sees us. Miss Pearce calls him in and says, 'Tópé was very upset in the playground this morning, Mr Gordon. I'm just popping to get some tissues, as someone has finished what was in the box, and a nice cup of cool water for Tópé. You might want to find out a bit more.'

Mr Gordon looks like a giant as he stands over our heads and says, 'So lads, do you want to explain?'

My voice can't make any words and my mouth is upside down.

Femi answers, 'Tópé is not feeling well, Mr Gordon.'

Mr Gordon replies, 'I'm sorry to hear this, Tópé. You can rest in here for a while. Femi, you can stay with Tópé until he's better if you want. I'll let your teachers know where you are. If you're still unwell after resting we can call home, okay?'

Femi says, 'Joe upset him, Mr Gordon.'

'What do you mean?' asks Mr Gordon.

'He said he's a weirdo,' Femi says.

'Was there anyone else involved?' Mr Gordon asks.

'Sean's usually all right, but he said Tópé was weird too,' Femi says reluctantly.

Miss Pearce comes back in with a cup of water and a box of tissues.

'I'll have to speak with both of them, I'm afraid. Miss Pearce, would you be kind enough to ask Joe and Sean to come to the Rainbow Room immediately, please, so that I can speak to all four boys together,' Mr Gordon says in a stern manner.

Mr Gordon turns back to me, shaking his head, and says in a gentler voice, 'Tópé, I'm really sorry to hear all of this, but don't worry – we will sort it.'

I don't know where to look, so I close my eyes. Right now I wish I was hiding in the little wooden hut in Nigeria with Abi. Back home things like this were not a problem.

I can see Joe and Sean walking towards us. As they enter the room with their heads bowed down, Mr Gordon starts on them. 'How have you been treating Tópé in the playground, Joe?' asks Mr Gordon.

Joe gives Femi and me a real bad look, as if to say, 'You wait! Just wait!' but he doesn't answer Mr Gordon.

'Sean, do you have anything to say, since nothing has been said so far?' Mr Gordon asks.

Sean starts scratching his head with his left hand and has a puzzled look on his face.

Mr Gordon says in a loud voice, 'Boys, can I have an answer, please? How would you feel if you started school in Nigeria and everyone made fun of you?'

Sean's face goes all pink and his glasses steam up, so I can't see his eyes properly, then he says, 'I'm sorry, Mr Gordon.'

'Sorry for what, Sean?' asks Mr Gordon.

'For being horrible to Tópé. I didn't mean to hurt his feelings, honest,' Joe says looking at Mr Gordon's brown shoes.

'Shouldn't it be Tópé you are apologising to and not me?' asks Mr Gordon.

'I... I... I'm sorry Tópé,' says Sean, looking at me, even though I still can't see his eyes properly through his foggy glasses. I look into his face not knowing whether to smile at him or not.

'And Joe, do you have anything to say, because from what I've heard you have been disrespectful to Tópé? You should already be aware that we do not accept such rudeness,' says Mr Gordon.

Joe twiddles his fingers and, in a feeble voice I can just about hear, he says, 'I'm sorry, Tópé.'

'I think you are going to have to do better, Joe,' fumes Mr Gordon. 'Look up when you are speaking, lad, and speak clearly.'

Finally, Joe says in a louder voice, 'I'm really sorry, Tópé and Femi.'

'Right! Can we say that this will be the last of this offensive behaviour?' Mr Gordon asks.

'Yeah,' Joe replies.

'Yeah who?' Mr Gordon asks.

'Yes, Mr Gordon,' Joe says.

Mr Gordon tells Sean and Joe to stand outside his office for twenty minutes, and Femi goes back to his classroom. I drag my feet to the dinner hall where I see Terry and Randall and go to lunch with them. I'm still not used to the strange smell in the dinner hall, but I do manage to eat a little pasta. Then I see Joe enter the dining room and he gives me a blank look, which I cannot figure out.

At afternoon break we all play a game of football in the playground. I score two goals, one of which is a really tricky shot, and Sean scores one. I wonder if Joe is okay now because he doesn't say much. I move in between Sebastian and Joe and manage to dribble the ball from between the two of them and take full control, but then the bell goes and we have to go back to our classrooms. Sebastian calls to me as we are walking off and says, 'Tópé, you have got to join the after-school football club.'

And Sean turns and says, 'Yeah, I hope you do, Tópé.'

Femi continues with, 'Yeah, it's really good fun, and our school team has won a place in the London Junior League Champions tournament, which is coming up soon.'

I smile and say, 'Yes, okay,' but then notice Joe looking at me from the corner of his eye and he isn't smiling, but then he looks at Femi and says, 'Can't Sean and me still come to your party, Femi?'

'All right,' he answers, 'but lay off Tópé.'

We all head for our classrooms. Miss has split us into groups, and me, Randall, Grace and Samantha work on a Viking project until it's time to go home again.

When my class follow Miss and go outside to the playground we wait to get picked up, I look up and spot Aunty chatting on her mobile by the gates, with Happy jumping up and down at her side. Femi is already with them. Miss Turner sees Aunty, so she says, 'Tópé, you can go now. Have a good weekend.'

I say, 'Thanks, Miss Turner,' and then rush off through the busy playground. I wish my mum and dad were at the school gates.

Football Tournament

It has been two weeks since I got into the after-school club and time has rushed by and today is the day. I feel so lucky to be playing in the tournament as I've only been with the school team for a couple of weeks. Terry and Randall from my class didn't get picked for the team to play in the tournament, but Mr Da Costa said I was excellent at football and that I could play centre forward.

'Come on, Tópé. It's Saturday, tournament day,' Femi says as he opens the curtain and the sun shines in my face.

'Mind my boat. You just pushed it,' I say stretching my arms out to stop it wobbling.

'Sorry. I hope you haven't got up in a bad mood. Why is the boat so precious anyway? Was it your mum or dad's?'

'Yes,' I say.

'Oh! You should have said.'

'My mum gave it to me as a present.'

'Oh, I understand now, Tópé. It must have taken ages to do. I'd love to be able to make a boat like this,' says Femi and he puts his face right near to the boat.

'My dad used to joke and say three of the people were me and him and Mum.'

'Which three?'

'Where there's two missing, and that's me in the middle.'

'But where are your mum and dad?'

'I don't know,' I say, shrugging my shoulders.

'Uh oh! Look at the time,' says Femi looking at the red clock on the wall. 'We need to pack our football gear fast and go and meet Mr Da Costa and the guys outside the community centre,' he says and pulls up his football socks. 'And what are you doing with your football at the end of the bed again? I thought I told you already.'

I ignore him.

When we are ready, we knock on the bedroom door and say goodbye to Aunty and Happy. Uncle has already left for work to do his Saturday morning shift, so he wished us good luck before we went to bed last night.

'Good luck, boys, but do take care and don't be late,' calls Aunty.

We soon reach the community centre. The others are already there waiting outside the centre, and a blue mini-bus is parked up nearby. Mr Da Costa waves at us to come over.

''Morning, boys. Good to see you,' he says. 'Fit and ready, are we?'

Femi and I nod with big smiles, and then we go over and stand next to Sean and Sebastian.

Sebastian is doing kick-ups on the spot with his ball and just nods his head at us, with his curly hair waving about. Sean is fiddling with his glasses, trying to clean them with his top, and Joe is kicking a stone about.

We all huddle into the blue mini-bus and Mr Da Costa drives off.

As we drive along, I see so many big red double-decker buses, with people sitting upstairs and downstairs. In Nigeria, we have all different-coloured buses, and also the Danfo and Molue buses in Lagos that are yellow, but they are not double-deckers. Our bus slows down, as there are more and more cars. I spot loads of people marching along with banners, but I can't make out the writing on them.

'We'll never get there at this speed,' moans Sebastian.

'Yeah, looks like it's a go-slow,' I say.

'A what, Tópé?' asks Sean.

'Oh, it's like a huge pile-up of vehicles,' explains Femi.

'A what?' Sean asks again.

'It's when there are lots of cars and you don't move very fast in the traffic. That's what we call it in Nigeria,' I say. 'Plus lots of street sellers come and try to sell things to people on the bus when you stop.'

'Oh,' says Sean, 'a traffic jam. Go-slow sounds good.'

Joe stands up and starts messing about, then he shouts 'GO!' on the spot and then quietly says, 'Slow!'

'Sit down, Joe. Less noise please, and do your seatbelt up,' says Mr Da Costa, looking in the mini-bus mirror at us in the back.

'That's the London Eye, Tópé,' says Femi, pointing.

'Where? I can't see an eye.'

'That big round thing, there.' Femi points again.

'Oh! I see,' I say. But it doesn't look much like an eye. It's more like a big wheel. They have funny names for things in England.

We drive on further for a good while then Mr Da Costa says, 'Here we are, lads.' I look out of the mini-bus window and can see where we are going to play. Lots of other coaches and mini-buses arrive and I can see loads of other teams. Some of the other teams are jumping up and down together. I wonder if it is because they want to keep warm as it is quite cold today. Some of the teams are in green and yellow, some wear just blue and some wear red and white striped tops. We are in black and white. I feel nervous since I've never played football in a tournament in England before.

As we pull into our parking space, I see two really big-built boys kicking each other, and another two look like they are having a fight near to the wooden changing huts. In our crowded mini-bus we look at each other with worried expressions.

'Come along, boys. All off the mini-bus and into the changing-rooms as quick as you can,' orders Mr Da Costa. 'You need to get ready for the first match.'

Once we are out of the changing rooms, Mr Da Costa gets us all in a circle and says, 'Look now, lads, keep professional and play by the rules. Don't feel intimidated, and give each match your best shot today, okay? Remember, we play to win.'

We all listen carefully. I bite my nails.

The first match is an easy game. I do a fantastic scissor kick and jump high in the air, kicking the ball until it falls back and over my head at Sebastian's feet. Joe uses some fancy footwork and, for once, closes his mouth and lets his feet do the talking to score the winning goal.

The second and third games are harder, but we just manage to get our place in the final.

Our final match will be the toughest because the team we are up against have won the trophy for the last three years. By half time we are losing by 5-4 and the goals we have scored have been really lucky. It doesn't look like we can win. It has started to rain and I think we are the losers.

We all pile back on to the field after a miserable half-time break. 'Come on now, lads, this is your last chance,' Mr Da Costa shouts. 'Boost it up a bit.' And I have a twinkle of thought and remember some of my mother's words: 'If there's no trying then there's no succeeding.' I take a very deep breath and decide to really go for it.

Femi dribbles the ball and ducks and darts between a gigantic boy on the other team. He's fast, but the other player is pushing into him and trips him up. The referee blows the whistle and shouts, 'Deliberate foul! Cut the rough stuff!' The other team member is sent off. This is the turning point for me. I feel a wave of confidence and keep thinking of my mum in Nigeria and how she always wanted me to try my best, but also Femi who stood up for me against Joe.

Sean passes to me and Sebastian shouts, 'Nutmeg him, Tópé!' So I pass the ball through my opponent's legs and run round him to take charge again. I then roll the ball along and make it look as if I'm going to pass it back to Sean or over to Joe then, just as they think I'm going to pass it, I do a dummy and kick it all the way down the slithery, sludgy grass. I go for it all the way down to the goalpost, then give a cruel kick and POW!

All my mates crowd me and we slap about playfully in the mud. Cheers come from not only my mates, but also the people watching, and then I hear Mr Da Costa say, 'Well done, lad.'

The game is far from over and we need another goal to win.

Sean gets a clearing from Joe and smoothly exchanges a pass with Femi. A defender who is waving his arms around is on Femi's case, but Femi zooms forward and his feet work like magic on the sliding pitch. Luckily, he eventually manages to pass the ball to Sebastian.

Someone in the crowd shouts, 'Belt it in.'

Then, just when it looks as if we have almost nailed it, one of our opponents tackles Sebastian's left side and has firm control of the ball. I move in fast and try to take charge, but one of the other players puts his foot between mine and SPLAT! I go thud, crashing on my knees in the mud. My left knee is in agony, but I quickly get up and I see the crowd has eyes on me, but I feel like dropping back in the mud.

The whistle goes and I hear the referee shout, 'Foul! Free kick!'

'I'll do it,' I say firmly.

'Are you sure after that fall, lad?'

Then Joe pipes up with, 'I always take the free kicks.'

I look at Joe and say, 'We're on the same team.'

'But your team mate has already said he'd like to,' says the referee to Joe. 'And anyway, there's no time for chat now. Come on, lads.' He continues looking at me, then he repeats, 'You sure?'

I nod yes, firmly.

I look at Joe then Femi and Mr Da Costa, and then I glance at the crowd. I say firmly to the referee, 'I'll do the free kick.' My left knee is stinging, but I have to do this. I turn around facing the crowd. All eyes are on me. To my right, Joe sneers at me angrily. Sean and Sebastian on my left are breathing heavily and Femi gives me the thumbs up. I take a deep breath and position myself. This is it. I take one heated, heavy shot and chip the ball over the goalkeeper. And there it is, in the net – Goal! Score!

'Boo!' I can hear the rival's supporters shouting. But our supporters roar even louder and I can hear 'Tópé! Tópé! Tópé!' We have won the tournament!

Mr Da Costa says, 'Well done, lads, you did it!' He taps me on my back and continues with, 'If I'm honest, I had my doubts. But you were amazing. This is a great day. We must celebrate, and Tópé scoring those last two goals really nailed it.' He punches the air, giving us all a big smile. 'Once we return, I'll buy some drinks and food at the shop round the corner from the community centre and then we can celebrate properly before you go home.'

'Yeah, we do need to celebrate like a proper football team, don't we?' says Sebastian with a big smile on his face. 'Why don't we get some chips from the chippy?'

'Yeah, let's,' I say.

'But you can't stand the smell of the chips in the school dinner hall, Tópé,' says Femi.

'Yeah, well, I quite like them now.'

'Whatever you want, boys – my treat,' says Mr Da Costa.

'If Tope wants chips today, he has chips because he helped us win the tournament this time,' says Sebastian.

'Yeah, you are right,' says Sean.

As we are about to reach the bus, my team lift me on to their shoulders and start singing, 'We are the champions! We are the champions!'

Today, I feel like a hero.

Special Things

Lying in my bed, I feel really excited about winning the tournament and also that Femi is having his party tomorrow, but I just wish that I could tell my mum and dad about everything that has happened of late. I step out of bed and decide to pull my suitcase from underneath my bed. I haven't looked through it for the last two weeks. I don't switch the light on because Femi might wake up, so I guide myself underneath my bed using my hands. Some dust flies into my mouth and I put my finger to my nose to stop myself sneezing. Finally, I feel the case and pull it out. I touch all of the objects that are still in there. I took out my clothes and everyday things when I arrived, but the special things are still here. First, I find the tie that my dad used to wear to church. I can still smell my dad on it and I place the tie loosely around my neck. Then there is my mum's handkerchief; I can smell her so strongly too, as if she's with me. I place it inside my pyjama pocket on the left side of my chest. It's a warm feeling. I then fumble about for my mum's wedding ring and put it on my biggest finger, even though it is far too big for me so it wobbles. I continue to feel inside the case for the other things and carefully pick up the newspaper cuttings and photographs of my mum and dad, which I can just see in the dim light. I come out from underneath the bed and kiss my dad's tie goodnight, then rub my mum's handkerchief over my cheeks. I decide to transfer all of the special things in to my shoebox because they will fit neatly in there and I can keep them in my own private place. I am extra careful in the dark with the papers. I put the lid on and gently place it back underneath my bed where no one can see it.

I have a good sleep and wake up feeling better than I have since moving to England, and today is Femi's tenth birthday. Now I know that if I feel sad in the night, I can take out my special box so that I can be near my mum and dad again and just smell them a little. This is about me and the box, and me and the box only – and of course my mum and dad if they are looking down on me. I suppose it's not their fault that there was a crash and they died.

Femi jumps out of bed and shouts with two fists above his head, 'Yes! I'm ten now – double figures – and the same age as you now, Tópé.'

'Don't forget I'm still older though, Femi, and in the next year at school.'

As I go downstairs, I see that Aunty and Uncle have bought a big green cake. It has a black and white football in the middle, with silver writing that says, 'Happy Birthday Femi.' Ten white candles are stuck around the circle of the football. The cake is sitting right in the middle of the big table to the back of the sitting room and surrounded by lots of other pretty little bits of cold food that are covered in see-through plastic. Aunty says that she needs to wash and dress Happy and that we must eat some breakfast, then get ourselves sorted; the party guests are due to arrive for 10am.

Before we finish getting dressed the doorbell goes and we both dash out of the bedroom, but Uncle stops us and says, 'No, sorry, boys. You need to dress first and pack your swimming bags. I will see your friends in.'

As we finish getting ready the doorbell goes two more times. When we reach downstairs the doorbell goes again and it is Aunty Ajoke. She has come with a big pot of jollof rice and some stew in another container. She says, 'Happy birthday, birthday boy and young Tópé. Let me go and see Aunty and Happy and put these heavy pots down in the kitchen before we speak properly.'

Joe, Sean and Sebastian are sitting in the front room. We all say hello to each other then Uncle says we have to leave or we will be late for the swimming party session. We all head out of the front door with our swimming bags, down the garden path to get in the car. Aunty Ajoke takes her car, too.

The swimming pool is massive. We quickly get changed and get into the pool. Aunty and Aunty Ajoke sit at some tables and watch, and Uncle takes Happy in the really shallow end with her pink armbands around her arms.

'Ah! It's freezing!' shouts Sebastian as he jumps in.

'I'm diving,' says Joe, and he splashes into the pool.

A whistle blows and the lifeguard calls over to us, 'Sorry, no diving in the pool.'

I put my right foot in and feel the water as I hold on to the metal steps leading down. Yuck! It is so cold. Sean jumps in and so does Femi. I have no choice, so I walk backwards down the steps into the coldness slowly and shiver.

'Come on, boys, you only have an hour in the pool,' says Uncle.

'I bet you can't touch the ground in the deep end,' Joe says to me.

Uncle must have heard him and says, 'No, sorry, boys. You must keep this side of the pool where you can always stand up and the water comes only as far as your shoulders.'

We start swimming around and having great fun, then we all try and do handstands in the water and count who can do the most. I do seven, Sebastian and Sean do eight, Joe does nine, and Femi does ten.

'Ten for your age, Femi,' I shout out as we continue to splash about.

Happy starts to cry, then Uncle says, 'Come on, boys, time's up. You need to come out now.'

Happy always spoils the fun.

After we are all showered and changed, we head back home and eat loads of food, then sing Happy Birthday to Femi. We all laugh together because he can't blow out his candles. I start to feel really tired so I sit on the settee next to Happy and just stare at the cartoons on the television. Femi and his mates head upstairs to play in our bedroom. I can't even be bothered to follow them. Aunty Ajoke, Aunty and Uncle are chatting loads in the kitchen. Eventually everyone goes home and what is left of the day seems to disappear.

When it is bedtime, Femi and I wearily walk upstairs to our bedroom. Aunty pops her head around the door to say goodnight, but turns a bit mad because our room is in a complete and utter mess. We even had to crawl around the mess to get to our beds. She soon stops huffing and puffing though, calms down a bit and then says, 'Please sort this mess when you are home from school tomorrow, boys.'

The following day at school we are all messing around in the playground.

Usually my classmates and Femi's eat separately, but today is different. For once, we can all sit together for lunch in the sports hall because there is a meeting being held in the dinner hall this afternoon.

Mr Bearsden, the science teacher, joins us at our table. When he stands up to get his afters and a cup of tea, my mate Randall looks at me and says, 'Let's pour salt in the sugar container – quick, before he comes back.' I hesitate, thinking it's not a nice thing to do, but then Randall says, 'Okay, if you won't do it, Tópé, you do it, Sean.'

'Oh go on, you chicken, Sean,' Joe says. 'Just because Tópé's a goody two shoes, we don't all have to be.'

I begin to feel small, like I've let my mates down. And I've been trying so hard to fit in.

Sean quickly opens the bottom of the sugar container and pours it into a spare cup on our table. He opens the salt container and pours the contents into the empty sugar container. He quickly puts the cup with the sugar in it on the windowsill. Mr Bearsden returns and plonks himself down in the tiny chair, which he bulges over. We all dash off giggling to the playground to play football.

'Go on Tópé, score – belt it in now!' Randall calls. But just as I'm about to kick an amazing shot in the goal, I hear Mr Bearsden shouting at us from the far end of the playground.

'You lot playing football over there – here now!'

I want desperately to shoot, but he repeats himself and sounds really angry, just like when Mr Fashakin used to get mad at us in Ibadan. I guess angry teachers are the same everywhere in the world.

Mr Bearsden takes us to his classroom and lines all seven of us up, facing him. 'Who thought it was funny to put salt in the sugar container today?' he begins angrily. 'Or was it a joint effort, so I should punish all of you?'

I keep my head down and don't smirk like the others, but I move about a bit and can't keep my feet still. I don't know where to look. No one says anything. Joe twiddles with his fingers, and I keep a straight face. I finally look up at my mates and they all have strange expressions on their faces, except Femi who is frowning at me.

'Right! Let me go and find Mr Gordon and we can all discuss this together. Then you can wipe those dirty smirks from your faces. I'll let your class teachers know where you are. You can lose your afternoon break time for all I care,' Mr Bearsden growls, then he heads out the door to fetch the head teacher.

We all stand still for a moment and do nothing, but then Sean, who is standing closest to Mr Bearsden's desk, says, 'Look, he's left his fancy watch on his desk – should be worth a bit that.'

'Take it, Sean,' Joe says.

'Yeah, grab it, Sean,' Randall says.

'I'll nick the watch,' Randall says, 'or do you want to do it, Tópé?'

'Me?' I ask, surprised.

'Just grab it,' says Joe.

'But I can't,' I say.

'You're such a chicken, Tópé. Just grab it. We haven't got all day,' says Randall.

'But why me?' I ask.

'Because you never do anything daring,' says Randall.

I start to feel confused. I know I don't want to take Bearsden's watch, but the pressure from my friends is heavy and I want them all to like me. In a faint voice I say, 'I can't do it.' But then as I look up and see everyone's eyes on me, I feel I have no choice other than to act. I swoop up the watch as fast as I can and clasp it tight in my hand. Then, in a swift movement, I stuff it in my trouser pocket. I feel like I've just picked up a time bomb and that the countdown started the moment my fingers touched it.

'Bearsden's coming! Stand still!' says Randall as Mr Bearsden walks into the room. Then, at that same moment, the bell goes.

Mr Bearsden looks all red and hot and comes out with, 'Okay, count yourselves lucky this time. Mr Gordon is dealing with another incident. But I'll be keeping an eye on all of you.' His eyes beam into our faces. 'Now go back to your classrooms.'

Terry, Randall and I go back to our classroom and the others go with Femi to theirs. As I sit in class that afternoon I feel like I cannot breathe properly. Miss Turner asks me three times if I'm okay. Each time I say the same words, 'Yes thanks, Miss.'

After what feels like many hours, the afternoon bell goes and it makes me jump. I wonder if I should try and put the watch back, but too many people are about. Terry has already gone with the after-school club, but I catch up with Randall and whisper, 'What should I do with it, Randall?'

'Nothing to do with me, Tópé. Don't know what you are talking about,' he says before dashing off.

When we reach home, Femi says to me, 'We can get into big trouble with that watch in the house, Tópé.'

'I wanted to put it back but too many people were around. I don't know what to do.'

'But shouldn't we put it back?' asks Femi.

'Yes, but how?' I ask.

'I don't know,' answers Femi. 'But we had best go downstairs to Mum because she will wonder what we are doing up here for so long. You know she always susses it when we are up to something.'

'I'll stuff it under my pillow for now,' I say.

We all eat dinner together and watch a bit of television. Then Femi and I do our homework in the living room before bedtime, but we keep glancing at each other.

Happy goes to bed first because she's the youngest. Then Femi and I go soon after. I want to talk to Femi about the watch, but as soon as his head hits his pillow he's in a deep sleep, snoring with his eyes half-open. I lie in the dark, thinking. I can hear ticking in my head. I make a bit of noise in the bedroom, hoping Femi will notice, but he doesn't stir. The ticking seems to be growing louder and louder. Finally, I lift my pillow and see the watch glaring at me in the dark. What should I do? I need to get it away from my pillow and my head. I decide to hide it away behind my special box for the night, so I pick it up, climb underneath my bed and reach for my box. I reach and reach, again and again, but my fingers hit the wall and the skirting board and all I can feel is dust – loads of it.

I start to panic. I want desperately to switch the light on, but then Femi will know about my special possession. I slowly pull my torch out of my drawer. My football falls to the floor and bounces, but Femi does not stir. I shine the torch under the bed – Nothing.

I don't know what to do, as no one else knows about this. Bits of my mum and dad have gone. Something of mine has been stolen. Where can it be? My box is all I have left of my mum and dad.

I begin to cry then fling my pillow on the floor. I bow my head low and don't know what to do. I think about Mr Bearsden missing his watch and me missing my special box. I so wish I had not taken it.

I hear Aunty and Uncle going to bed and then all of the lights go out, until even the bit of light that filters through the gap of my bedroom door from the landing is gone.

I lie on the floor, put my head on my pillow and go to sleep crying.

I wake up early the next morning when Femi nearly treads on me as he gets up.

'Why are you sleeping on the floor, Tópé?' he asks.

'I've lost something – something very special to me,' I say.

'What? You never told me you had anything special,' he replies with his eyebrows raised.

'My special box,' I say.

'What special box? What does it look like?' he asks, looking puzzled.

'The shoebox that my new shoes came in. I didn't throw it away and kept it for something...' I trail off.

'Oh that! Here it is,' Femi says, opening the wardrobe door. 'When I had my party I saw Sean with it and told him to keep off our things, and then locked it away in here. I didn't know it was so special.' Femi hands me my box and it is at that moment that I know what I have to do.

We arrive at school early and I go straight to Mr Bearsden's classroom with Femi. We both look around to make sure that no one is watching us. Nobody is there, so we sneak up to the door and peek in. The coast is clear, so we open the door and walk towards Mr Bearsden's desk to put the watch back. I'm so relieved.

I'm just about to put the watch down, when I hear Mr Bearsden's loud voice behind me. 'And what, may I ask, are you two doing in here?'

'Err...! Umm...! Err...!' I say sheepishly as I look up at Mr Bearsden.

He then spots the watch and says, 'What are you doing with my watch?'

'Err...! Umm...! Err...!' I say.

'Well well! We have a culprit. Femi, can you explain?'

'We didn't mean to take it, Mr Bearsden, and we are very sorry,' says Femi.

I stare at a science poster on the wall then say, 'Yes, we are very sorry. Honest, Mr Bearsden.'

'Do you know what that watch means to me? Do you know how special it is? My grandfather bought me that watch before he passed away. I'm not happy,' he says angrily.

He pauses for a moment and then continues. 'Do you know you two are very lucky because I was going to call the police? But as you have apologised and were quite clearly putting my precious watch back, I will once again let you off.' Then his face and his yellow and grey beard comes right near us and he says, 'If I have to talk to you a third time for the rest of this term it will be serious, and Mr Gordon will surely be involved!'

The morning bell goes and Mr Bearsden says, 'Now off with you, and keep out of trouble – or else!'

Once we are in the hall, I say, 'I wish I hadn't taken his watch, Femi.'

'Yeah, stealing is bad,' says Femi.

'I know. I was just trying to fit in,' I say.

'Real friends aren't going to want you to do things you don't want to, Tópé.'

'Next time I won't,' I say firmly.

I think my mum and dad would be so mad at me if they ever knew.

I miss them so much.

Sleepover

'Yes, Mrs Buxton, I've already put their sleeping bags in the boot,' Aunty says. 'I hope they all behave themselves for you. They're just having some dinner, then we will leave.' Aunty puts the phone down from speaking to Joe's Nan.

It's Friday evening of a Bank Holiday weekend. Joe's Nan has invited us to stay over for two nights and asked if we could help tidy up her garden. It's Joe's Great-Nan really, but he calls her Nan. Joe will be there, of course, and so will Sebastian and Sean. This is my first time staying at someone's house in England.

Femi and I pack up a bag each with our toothbrushes, a change of clothes, pyjamas and, more importantly, football cards and my football from Nigeria.

'Bye Uncle! Bye Happy!' I say as Femi and I get in the car with Aunty.

'Enjoy your weekend, boys,' calls Uncle. He's holding Happy as she thumps his chest and pulls away. It looks like she wants to come, too.

I grin until my cheeks hurt, but then, as I look out the window, I think about being at Joe's Nan's house and hope he's not horrible to me when I'm there; he still barely speaks to me. I look out and see lots of different coloured lights shining everywhere and lots of buildings everywhere. I see a restaurant that says 'Best Fast Food – Nigerian Suya.'

We soon reach Joe's Nan's house and see her standing at the door in a pink dressing-gown, wearing glasses that point at the top edges. She smiles and waves to us as we park. Then Joe pops his head round her side.

Aunty speaks to Mrs Buxton at the doorway for a while then says goodbye to us all and leaves.

We go through a narrow hallway with lots of photographs on the wall.

'Joe, it's getting late. Show your friends upstairs so that they can put their bags and sleeping bags down,' Mrs Buxton says.

We go up the stairs with Joe leading the way. Sean and Sebastian have arrived before us and are already upstairs in one of the spare bedrooms.

Mrs Buxton follows us upstairs and pokes her head in the door. 'You can have a drink of hot chocolate and a couple of my special biscuits before bed. I don't want you all up too late because there's a lot to be done in the garden tomorrow. And not too much noise; Simon and Vashtee next door have a new baby.'

'Okay, Nan,' says Joe.

'I hope you boys are not too squashed in here, but as you have insisted on camping on the floor in one room instead of using the other spare room, I suppose that's that.' Mrs Buxton takes her glasses off and rubs her eyes. 'Goodnight, boys. I'm turning in now, as I'm very tired. Sleep well,' she yawns, and shuffles off in her fluffy slippers to her bedroom.

The minute she shuts our door Joe flings his pillow in my face. I chuck it back at him. Then Joe picks up two pillows and throws them in the air. Sean grabs one and hurls it at Femi, and Sebastian grabs the other and tosses it in Joe's face. We all start cracking up with laughter. I can't stop giggling. Then we fling the pillows all over the room and feathers start flying around.

'Ouch! Your fingernail just scratched my arm, Sean,' says Sebastian.

'Big baby! Sebastian is a baby!' the rest of us start singing.

Sebastian looks angry and goes to sit down on a wicker chair in the corner of the room. I feel bad at joining in because Sebastian has always been kind to me. I stop singing.

Mrs Buxton opens the bedroom door and comes back in. 'Come on now, boys,' she says then she notices Sebastian in the corner. 'Cheer up, Sebastian. I know it can be frightening sleeping away from home, but I'm only in the next bedroom,' she says, and then she closes the door.

'Your Nan doesn't really get it does she, Joe?' Femi says.

'Ah well! Never mind,' says Joe.

It gets late and we all eventually nod off, one by one.

I wake up and see that my mates are already awake and swapping football cards. Mrs Buxton comes into the bedroom.

'Morning, boys. I've set the table for breakfast, but you've woken up so late it'll be more like a mid-morning snack. Help yourselves to cereal and toast, and I've just put a pot of tea on the table. Once you're sorted we must get cracking with that weedy, overgrown garden of mine. I'm so grateful that you have all come to help me.'

'We won't take long, Nan,' says Joe.

'I'm going to make a start, so I'll see you boys in the garden,' Mrs Buxton says as she makes her way to the back door in her flowery wellies and an overall.

We eat then wash and dress quickly, because we can't wait to go outside.

The garden is enormous. We run down to Mrs Buxton, who is cutting back a big bush.

'I thought I'd start at the back and work up, boys. Grab a pair of gloves each and a spade or fork and get cracking. But do be careful with the garden tools as they can be very dangerous,' instructs Mrs Buxton.

We all start digging and digging. It's really hard work, but fun, too. Then we use the rake to pull some of the weeds to one side. Loads of slimy worms come wriggling through the mud and Sebastian finds an ants' nest with tons of ants marching out.

'Boys! Let me go and make us all a cool drink, as you must be getting rather hot from this hard work. I think some lemon and barley water will do nicely,'

Mrs Buxton tells us and makes her way down the overgrown path to the house.

'Lemon and what water did your Nan say, Joe?' I ask.

'Oh, she means squash, Tópé, a kind of fancy one. My Nan says she only buys the best.'

'There's the man next door with the baby,' Sean says as he peers through a gap in the bushes.

'Forget about Simon next door and come and help me over here,' Joe calls out. 'My fork has got stuck.'

Sean ignores Joe and continues snooping on Simon and the baby. Sebastian and Femi join him.

I go to give Joe a hand and say, 'Let me have a try.' I use all of my power to move the fork, but it won't budge. Then I stand on top of it with my legs around the pole, but it still won't budge. 'I think we will have to dig with our hands, Joe,' I suggest, but all he does is open his hands to his side and shrug.

We both kneel down and start to pull away the weeds and the mud from between the fork prongs. There are lots of big jagged rocks and one of them catches Joe's wrist.

'Ouch!' he yelps. 'You and your digging. I'm not doing any more,' Joe says in a stroppy voice. 'I'm going to get my Nan to help us.'

He always gives up, I think to myself.

I continue digging with my hands and then I finally manage to loosen up the fork a bit. I stand up and pull at it, but notice that there's an odd-shaped object, the size of my fist, stuck between the fork prongs. I reach down to pull at it, but it is still stuck. It feels hard and uneven. I don't think it's a rock. I take off my gardening gloves and use my bare hands to dig the fork and the strange object out of the ground.

I've got it. I hold it in both of my hands and take a look. It is muddy and rusty and I try to make out its shape. It looks like a small pineapple, but without any leaves on top. I dig some of the mud off with my fingernails then fidget about with the opening bit on top.

Mrs Buxton is coming down the garden with a tray of drinks and Joe follows her. 'Come along, you boys by the hedge,' she calls. 'I don't think the neighbours would like it if they knew you were spying on them. Plus, we have work to do. Fetch a drink and then we can start again.' Then she turns to speak to me. 'Here we are, Tópé. You take first pick as you seem to be the hardest worker this morning. Lemon and barley water was a special rarity in World War II, you know.'

'Thanks, Mrs Buxton,' I say and reach out my hand for the glass, keeping the muddy pineapple object in my other hand.

'Your hands, Tópé. You will have to go and wash them before you have your drink, and what's that you've found? Treasure? Or have you found an egg from a nest?' she says.

I hold out my hand to show her what I've found. All of a sudden Mrs Buxton looks strange. The tray of drinks topples and splashes us all.

'Danger!' she screams.

'What?' asks Joe and turns pale.

She calms herself down, then in a shaky voice says, 'Tópé, please listen very carefully. I need you to slowly and gently put that hand grenade down.'

'Grenade?' I say with shock.

'Yes, Tópé, and you must do it as carefully as you can.'

I look up at Mrs Buxton then I look at the hand grenade and freeze, then, ever so gently, I place it on the ground.

'Now boys, we must dash to the house. I will have to call the police.'

We all run for the house. Mrs Buxton flaps her hands about and looks really red in the face.

We reach the back door and Joe shouts through his tears, 'Is it a bomb, Nan?' His eyes and mouth turn to circles.

'Not now, Joe,' she says, shaking her head.

When we enter the house, she locks the back door with the key and dashes to the phone where she dials 999. We all huddle around her.

'Police! Police!' she says frantically.

I begin to feel frightened and my mates look worried. Joe wipes his eyes.

Mrs Buxton explains, 'We've found a hand grenade at the bottom of my back garden and it could blow up at any moment. I've heard about these grenades left from the War!' She takes a breath, as if she's listening to someone replying, and then continues in a loud voice. 'Don't you tell me to calm down, young man. I've got children in the house. Yes, the address coming up on your system is correct.' She hangs up the phone and looks at all of us. 'Now, let me get my keys and my handbag. Come on, boys. Follow me through the front door, quick as you can.' As Mrs Buxton takes us out of the house, we hear a police siren in the distance.

When the police car arrives, Mrs Buxton waves to them.

A uniformed policewoman gets out of the car and comes over.

'It's a grenade, a grenade, I repeat myself.' Joe's Nan tells the policewoman.

'Could you all follow me this way,' the policeman says, and leads us further away from the house.

Another police car arrives and the policewomen and policemen knock on the neighbours' doors and ask them to come outside. A policeman is putting striped tape around the front garden of Mrs Buxton's house.

A tall policeman gathers everyone together at the front of the houses on the pavement and starts talking. 'We're going to have to cordon off the area for everyone's safety. Can you all come this way to the exclusion zone, please?'

'I'm awfully sorry about this,' says Mrs Buxton to the policeman.

'Not your fault at all. You did the right thing by calling us. The bomb disposal experts are here now, so we will let them take a look and assess the device.'

'What did it feel like finding the grenade, Tópé?' asks Femi.

'It was just hard and full of mud,' I reply, 'but I felt nervous when I had to place it gently on the ground.'

'Did you think it was going to blow us up?'

'Yeah, I did,' I say.

We follow Simon and Vashtee, the couple with the baby from next door. And an old man with a funny hat comes out of the other side of Mrs Buxton's house. Before long, there are hundreds of evacuated people on the street. There is lots of chatter. Mrs Buxton is telling everyone that I found the hand grenade and everyone starts to ask me questions.

'Did you panic when you found it, lad?' asks the old man with the funny hat.

'No,' I reply, 'I didn't know what it was.'

BANG! BANG! We all look up to the sky and see black smoke coming from Mrs Buxton's back garden.

The baby starts crying.

A policeman comes to speak to the crowd and says, 'Okay, we have dealt with the problem. It was, in fact, a live hand grenade with no pin, which means that it was highly dangerous. Thank you to, I believe, this young lad here, Tópé, for finding it.'

Everyone looks at me. At first I feel embarrassed, but then everyone starts to clap. I've never heard so many thank yous.

'Can I call my Uncle and Aunty and tell them about the grenade, Mrs Buxton?' I ask.

'Of course you can, Tópé. You've probably just saved our lives.'

'It wasn't just Tópé,' Joe bursts out. 'I was helping him dig and I got the fork stuck. It's always him, him, him! He thinks he can come here and take over everything. And he's even trying to be better than me at football.'

'Joe!' Mrs Buxton calls. 'Where did that outburst come from?'

'Well, it's not fair that he's good at more things than me,' snorts Joe. 'And he gets all the attention.'

'But I'm not,' I say.

'Oh, come on, boys. Okay, you are both heroes today and I'm grateful to both of you for almost saving our lives. Hopefully, you can sort out the football problems on the pitch. Now come on, boys, let's not spoil the rest of the day. And anyway, you should be working together because you both play for the same team. Now shake hands, the both of you, and promise me no more of this nonsense. I think you owe Tópé an apology, Joe.'

'I'm sorry,' Joe says, 'I don't mean to be horrible, it just happens.'

'Yeah, and don't forget we could have just died,' says Femi.

I look up to the sky and wonder if I might have seen my mum and dad again if I had died.

Star Youth Academy

It's the middle of August and school ended a few weeks ago. School holidays are boring in England because we just hang around the house and there is nothing to do. In Nigeria, I could go out and play all day with my friends. I so miss the big games of football in the compound. Aunty and Uncle seem to think that Femi and I are not old enough to do what we want. Last week, Femi and I wanted to go to the cinema together, but Aunty said no. My mum and dad never used to treat me like a baby.

It's Thursday morning. Femi is watching television and Aunty is upstairs getting Happy dressed. I sit at the bottom of the stairs in my pyjamas and stare at my feet. I look up because I can see someone approaching the house through the pane of glass in the middle of the front door. It's the postman. He stuffs a couple of brown envelopes through the letterbox and they drop to the floor. I leave them there and look through the glass again. Someone else approaches the door.

They put a small piece of yellow paper through the letterbox and it floats down near to me. I pick it up and read:

Star Youth Academy

Auditioning tomorrow at 11am

Venue: Neugreen Chain Area Community Centre

Looking for something 'unique'

COULD YOU BE THE LOCAL STAR?

For further details contact: 6543 1293711238767

or e-mail: neugreenchaincommcen@star.com

Just as I finish reading the flyer, Aunty comes down the stairs holding Happy's hand, so I have to move out of the way.

'Morning, Tópé. How are you doing?'

'I'm bored,' I reply.

'Oh Tópé. The day is young. Come on, cheer up. I'm sure we'll think of something fun to do. Is that the post you have there?'

'There are two envelopes that just dropped, Aunty,' I say as I hand them to her. Happy runs off into the front room. 'And this yellow sheet of paper came too,' I continue.

'What's that?' asks Aunty.

'It's about a Star Youth , and something being held tomorrow.'

'Well it looks a lot brighter and more interesting than these brown envelopes, doesn't it? Nothing but bills, bills, bills these days.' Aunty starts to flip through the letters and then looks at me. 'Would you like to go, Tópé?' she asks.

'I don't know, Aunty. I'm not sure what it is.'

'Ah, it's an audition,' Aunty says, 'like a test – a competition. Show the flyer to Femi and see what he thinks,' Aunty finishes.

I go into the sitting room and give Femi the piece of paper. 'Aunty wants you to read this, Femi.'

He just puts it down on the settee and says, 'In a minute, Tópé.' And he continues watching the television with Happy.

I sit down in the armchair and start thinking of Nigeria again. If I still lived there, I would go out and play with my friends, John, Edwin and Abi. I wonder what they are doing now. When we were tired of football, I would play ayo with each of my friends. Sometimes we would make the game out of an old egg carton and play it with stones or beans. Some of the grownups used to say we shouldn't play the game when it gets late. I was never sure why they used to say that though. I can't wait for next year when Abi comes to see me.

Happy jumps up and starts to walk in front of the television with her thumb in her mouth.

'Happy, move out the way,' Femi says impatiently.

Then she moves back to the settee and picks up the piece of paper and starts scrunching it up in her hand. The advertisements come on the television and Femi tries to take the yellow paper from Happy. I get up to help. Before we can get hold of it, she throws it and starts laughing as if she's the smartest little girl in the world.

'Happy. Don't do that!' I say.

Happy just starts saying, 'No! No! No!' And then she runs out of the sitting room.

I pick up the paper.

'What is it anyway, Tópé?' Femi asks.

'It's a sort of test competition. Aunty says it's something we could do in the holiday to do with singing and dancing.'

'Test? Forget that! We do enough tests at school,' answers Femi.

'Yeah, I don't like tests either,' I say to Femi, handing him the piece of paper, 'but there is a big prize for the winner, Femi, and I like winning things,' I say.

'Yeah, so do I,' says Femi. Then he continues, 'but, what exactly can we do?'

'I don't know, Femi. We'll have to think.'

Aunty comes back in the room with Happy in her arms and says, 'Auditioning is at 11am tomorrow, boys. I think you should try and come up with something. Give it a go.'

'But we haven't got enough time,' I say.

'Yeah and we can't learn to do something that quickly, can we?' says Femi.

'Excuses! Excuses! What am I going to do with you two?' says Aunty. 'Why don't you invite some friends over to help you? Make a group. Try and be more positive. I'm sure you will shine.'

'I think Joe's going to his Nan's this week. Sean has been grounded because he swore at his mum and maybe Sebastian has gone to Cornwall,' Femi says.

'I could call Terry from my class and see if he's interested,' I suggest. 'Let's try Joe, Sean and Sebastian too, just in case.'

Terry is keen to come and says his dad is going to drop him at ours. Then Femi calls his mates from his class. Joe isn't going to his Nan's until later in the week so his mum says he can come round, and Sean's mum says he can join us too, even though he was rude to her and she's not very happy with him.

'Well, it looks like you are set then, boys,' says Aunty.

'But once we figure out what we're going to do, where will we practise? If we do it in the living room Happy will just get in the way,' I complain.

'We can do it in the bedroom, Tópé,' Femi says.

Femi and I eat our cornflakes and toast fast, gulp down our orange juice, and go upstairs to start thinking about what we will perform at the auditions. Then the doorbell rings, so we fly downstairs. Terry and Sebastian arrive at the same time, followed quickly by Joe.

We all go upstairs where Femi and I tell them about the competition and how we need to come up with something fast.

Before Joe even stops to think he grabs my football from the bottom end of my bed and starts bashing it with his hands.

'Give me back my football, Joe,' I say and try to snatch it from him.

'All right, calm down, Tópé,' Joe says, pulling away.

'What's your problem, Joe?' asks Femi.

'It's only a football,' says Joe.

'Yes, and it's my football,' I say as I try to pull it back.

We pull against each other, pushing and tugging. Then my ball goes flying and Joe topples against the side table. My wooden boat is thrown across the room and the model people go flying around on the beds and on the floor.

'Now look what you've done!' I yell and I push Joe hard.

'Yeah, and look what you've just done; you've scratched my arm.'

Terry and Sebastian stand to one side with wide eyes and mouths.

Joe pushes me sideways and I crash into Femi's bed. We fall in a heap on the floor with Femi saying, 'Stop it! We'll be in trouble.'

Joe and I wrestle on the floor in a scuffle then Aunty barges in and shouts, 'Enough! Stop this fighting right now!'

Aunty manages to prise us apart as we gasp for breath. She holds me in one hand and Joe in the other, and says, 'What on earth is going on in here?'

'Tópé's scratched my arm,' Joe shouts out.

I can hear Happy calling Aunty from downstairs. Aunty says, 'Femi, please go down and check on Happy for me. In fact, Terry and Sebastian, why don't you go with Femi too?' I've never heard Aunty speak so strict before.

'It's Joe's fault,' I say. 'He tried to take my football and then he knocked my boat on the floor and all the people have gone all over the place,' I say with tears flowing down my cheeks. 'And I'd already lost my mum and dad.'

'Yeah, but I was only playing with the football,' says Joe, now also in floods of tears. 'And ever since he came here no one thinks I'm the best at football any more and he found the hand grenade in my Nan's garden. Plus, I haven't got a dad either because he died in the war in Afghanistan before I was born. So there!'

'Yeah, well my mum and dad died in Nigeria,' I yell, 'and I had to come here.'

'Boys! Stop, stop, please!' demands Aunty.

Then Uncle puts his head around the bedroom door and says, 'What is going on in here? Femi said you two boys have been fighting.'

'Indeed they have, Olu,' says Aunty to Uncle, 'and I don't know where to begin.'

'Happy is crying for you downstairs. Do you want me to talk with Tópé and Joe and you go and see to Happy?'

'Okay, Olu,' says Aunty as she leaves the bedroom, shutting the door behind her and shaking her head.

My mouth pouts out, my eyes narrow and I stand awkwardly and continue to cry. Joe stands twiddling with his fingers, moving from side to side on each of his feet. I look up at Uncle's face, but he doesn't look as mad as I thought he would at us. That smell comes to me as I continue looking at him – the aftershave he wore when he came to Nigeria for me – but then I snap back to looking at him.

'Now, you two, what has been happening? You both know that fighting is not good, don't you?'

'Yes, Uncle,' I say with tears still coming down my face.

'Yes,' says Joe nervously.

'Come on, boys,' Uncle says as he sits on my bed. 'Come and sit either side of me. Now, I'm not entirely sure what this is about, but I know you two have had little tussles since you began at your new school, Tópé, and haven't always seen eye to eye. But it would be good to try and talk this through and set things straight, even if you have to agree to disagree. And fighting is a no no.'

Joe tells Uncle how, before I came, he was the best at football, and now I seem to get all the attention. And he says how he wishes he had a dad, too. I talk about how I miss my mum and dad so much and that is why my football and the wooden boat are so important to me. They are things I brought to England with me from Nigeria and they remind me of my mum and dad and life in Nigeria.

'Do you know you two have more in common than you realise? You are both really good football players and have both had to deal with losing parents. In fact, your head teacher, Mr Gordon, has told me that you two are the best footballers in the school. Instead of fighting, you two could play even better together – no one could win against you two! Can I ask you both to stand up and shake hands? And will you promise me you will try and be kind to each other and that there will be no more fighting?

Joe looks at me and I look up at him. We both stand and put our hands out. We start slowly, but then we have a really good, strong handshake. I just know that it is a real handshake and we smile the widest smiles at each other as tears come down our eyes.

'Thank you, boys. Come on, dry your eyes and let's pick up the wooden boat and people. We can put them back in the boat together,' says Uncle.

'See, my mum and dad are still missing,' I say as we put the last of the wooden figures in place.

Uncle says, 'Tópé, I told you I used to make things out of wood when I was young, didn't I? I would like to suggest that I buy some wood and you, Joe and I replace the two missing wooden figures for the boat. What do you think about that?'

'Yes, I would like that, Uncle. But what about Joe? Can we make him a boat with a man inside who can be his dad too, or an aeroplane?'

Joe's eyes open wide and he looks surprised, but then his mouth gives a big smile.

'Of course we can. But for now you boys are supposed to be practising for the competition tomorrow. So let's sort that out first, and once you've finished we can begin.'

'Okay,' Joe and I both say together.

'Right, now do you want to go downstairs to your friends so that you can work towards the audition again, but this time peacefully?'

'Yes, Uncle,' I reply.

'Talking of wooden objects, follow me downstairs, boys as I think I have a good idea that you might like.'

'I think I know what you are talking about, Uncle,' I say.

The Dundun Drummers

'Here, why don't you work with the Dundun Drums? This should really wow the crowds and show the judges something different.' Uncle picks up two of the three drums that are sitting in the corner. I look at the drums deeply and remember playing them with my granddad and dad. When I first came to England, I didn't even want to touch them, but I think I am ready now, and I just know that Dad and Granddad would be proud of me.

'They're the strangest drums I've ever seen,' says Terry, laughing as usual, because he laughs at everything. 'Bit strange having string all around the sides. And it looks like animal skin on the top. I can't wait to have a go, though.'

'They look really good,' says Sebastian, turning towards me, 'but I can't figure out what we do with them.'

'My granddad and dad told me we have to put the drum belt on our shoulders and this will help us to support the drum,' I explain. 'I used to play the Sangban, but I've forgotten some of it now. Some people used to play them on the ground, but my granddad said they are not really meant to be played like that. The name of the curved drumstick is the opa. Many people call them talking drums, because they can imitate the Yoruba language, but I'm not too sure about that bit.'

'Well,' says Uncle. 'I think Tópé has explained it all. Who wants to start?'

'Me! Me!' shouts Femi.

'And me!' I call.

'Okay, Tópé, you take the Sangban Drum. And, Femi, you take the slightly smaller Kenkeni.' Uncle picks up the remaining drum and says, 'Which one of you boys wants to try the larger Doundounba Drum?' looking at Joe, Sebastian and Terry.

'Can I have a go, please?' asks Terry. 'But they look heavy.'

'I want a go, too,' says Joe.

'You can all have a go. Take it in turns,' says Uncle. 'But let Terry go first, as he asked first.'

'But, Uncle, there aren't enough drums for all of us to play on the day,' I say.

'Yes, you are right, Tópé,' says Uncle. 'We might have a problem with that. In fact, you know what? My brother has the same drums at his house. I'll go over to his house in Lewisham later and ask if we can borrow them. But you can practise on these ones for now.'

'We could call ourselves the Dundun Drummers,' I suggest, and everyone agrees.

'Follow what I do and see if you can get the beat,' Uncle continues. 'Or watch what Tópé does as he follows me.'

Aunty sits listening and Happy starts jumping up and down. For once, she isn't getting in the way.

Uncle starts chanting a few simple words and we follow, concentrating on the drumbeats. At first, it sounds silly and then it starts to sound like something, like music – good music. We are really getting in to it. Uncle is wicked on the drums.

'Right, boys, that's it. You are set! A bit more practising later and you'll have the audience bopping in their seats.'

Femi and I practise late into the evening with our friends. Then Uncle and Aunty drop Terry, Joe and Sebastian home. We stop at Uncle's brother's house and pick up the other drums so we all have one each.

The next morning we all arrive to find lots of people going in. A group of girls have all got bright pink dyed hair and they are all wearing pink jackets, and two boys are holding skateboards with loads of graffiti on them.

A security guard lets us all enter once we have filled out a form with our act name.

'They must be the judges, Tópé,' Femi says looking over at four people sitting behind desks to the right side of the stage.

A man with a ponytail and baggy jeans starts talking loudly from the middle of the stage, using a microphone. 'Good morning, everyone. My name is Gary and I'm organising this event. I'd like to welcome you all and wish you good luck for today. A score over 15 from the judges means you will perform in the main show. Good luck, everyone, and thanks for coming,' he finishes.

A girl group wearing silver outfits perform first. They are really awful and screech like cats. But they look very confident. Then a boy sings alone. He has a really good voice and the audience don't make a sound when he sings. Then the two boys we saw earlier come on using their skateboards as part of their act. They are good, but then one of them trips on his skateboard and he walks off in a huff. His friend follows him. We hear Gary say, 'Number four – The Dundun Drummers.'

We all get up. Femi, Terry, Joe, Sebastian and I carry our drums to the centre of the stage and strap them over our shoulders. My legs feel a bit like jelly. All eyes are on us. Femi looks sure of himself, so I try to follow him, but then I notice that they are all watching me, as if they are waiting to copy my drumming. Joe is watching my every move as if he needs to follow what I do. We all stand silent for a minute and then I realise that we do not have a plan for how to start. I decide to take the lead and tap out a beat. I notice to my left that Femi is following me and then I see Sebastian smile at me and he too starts drumming, as does Terry, moving his body slightly. Joe begins to dance and starts jumping around as he plays his drum, so I dance over to him and wave my drumsticks over his head and we catch each other's eyes. Joe starts nodding to the beat.

I look up and see Happy in Uncle's arms waving at us from the crowd. She's shouting, 'Femi! Tópé! Femi! Tópé!' Aunty stands smiling with her arms folded.

We start to beat the drums and chant in rhythm. At a certain point in our drumming, we quickly put our drums on the floor to the side and move into our short dance routine. I feel much more confident now, and Femi and I grin at each other. Joe winks at me as he dances, and Terry and Sebastian are well into it. We then quickly strap our drums on our shoulders again and Femi misses a few beats, and we all start to beat out of rhythm. I look up and see Uncle clapping out the timing for us. I start to follow him and, miraculously, we are back in tune.

When we have finished, I feel a rush of joy and we go and stand with the other competitors to the left-hand side of the stage. The audience is only half-full, but everyone starts clapping. I smile at my mates and they smile back.

Gary comes back on the stage and says, 'Would the judges now show their votes.'

All of the judges hold up cards with numbers, and Gary calls the name of each group. The girls in silver only score 13, and they storm off the stage. The boy singer scores 19 and the two boys with skateboards score only 7. Then it is our turn, and I bite my nails and glance towards Femi as we wait. The cards are up, and we have scored 19! That means we are definitely in for the main show. I punch the air and say, 'Yes!'

Gary says, 'See you at the main show in a couple of days, and good luck, boys.'

We all pile into the car laughing and giggling and Uncle says, 'I knew you could do it!'

For the next two days, Femi, our friends and I are so busy. We keep practising and practising. The drumming turns out to be great fun and I remember more of what my granddad and dad taught me to show my friends. I would do anything to have one of those days again in Nigeria. When they used to show me how to play the drums in Nigeria, I never wanted to listen much, but now I want to remember every beat.

The day of the show finally arrives and Uncle goes to pick up our friends so that we can all go together.

Femi and I dress in our brightest Buba and Sokoto, and Happy wears a little Buba and Iro.

When we arrive at the NeuGreen Chain Area Community Centre, there is a very long queue. We go in a side door with Uncle while Aunty and Happy go to sit in the audience. Uncle says, 'Good luck, boys,' and then goes to join them.

I start to feel nervous and my belly is doing twists. I bite my fingernails. Femi seems calm. I look at him and smile. Joe is pursing his lips and Sebastian and Terry are frowning.

A security guard directs us with others backstage through a dim, thin passageway. It's a little scary, and for a minute I want to go home, but I tell myself not to be silly.

We listen as two groups go on ahead of us, while we wait behind a very big curtain. Then we hear Gary say, 'The next act is the Dundun Drummers. Please give them a warm welcome.'

As we walk out on to the stage, I look up, and though it's difficult to see everyone in the audience, it sounds like hundreds of people are clapping. My tummy starts to twist again. I've never seen so many people in front of me like this before. I look at Femi and he smiles at me again, but he, too, looks nervous now.

'Okay, you may begin, boys,' Gary says from the side of the stage.

Femi hits his drum then he looks at me. For a second, I freeze then, as Femi smiles at me, I start beating my drum and Terry follows me. Sebastian is drumming and smiling too, but then I notice that Joe looks really worried on the stage and everything goes quiet. I look up at the massive crowd with all eyes on us. I quickly go over to Joe, who is the other side of Femi, and whisper in his ear, 'Come on, we have to win this so we can make our boats.' Joe grins at me and I smile a wide smile.

Joe hits a beat and he comes into tune with the others and me. He continues to smile and we're back drumming again. The drums sound like they are talking with their own words and, as we continue to beat, it sounds harmonious. Next, we take the straps over our heads, put our drums down and do our dance routine. We all move in rhythm, three steps to the right and clap twice, then march on the spot five times and step three steps to the left. We then quickly pick up our drums and finish our performance.

I notice the people in the audience are all smiling and nodding their heads to the rhythm, and we get the loudest applause from the crowd I have heard. A few people are standing up and shouting, 'More! More! More!'

Uncle, Aunty and Happy are waving like mad at us.

Gary walks out on to the stage and speaks into his mike. 'Okay! Okay! Thank you, but we have two more acts yet, so if you could all take to your seats.'

As we walk off the stage, Joe turns to me and quietly says, 'Thanks for helping me out on stage, Tópé.'

'That's okay,' I reply.

We are all hot and go backstage to sit down again. 'That was wicked,' I say.

'Yeah, that was good,' says Joe, smiling at me.

The final two acts go on and then it's time for the winners to be announced. We sit behind the curtain backstage, waiting to hear the results.

An official-looking man in a red robe, with a big gold chain and frilly white fabric around his neck, walks by us and then we hear Gary talking in the microphone again. 'The local Mayor has come to announce the winners on what has been an amazing night tonight. I will hand the microphone over.'

'Good day, Star Youth Academy guests. I can now announce the winners, who are also the most unique of all the performers. Please give a round of applause to... the Dundun Drummers.'

I can't believe that we have won! We are led on to the stage. The crowd is roaring and clapping like crazy. Aunty and Uncle are spinning around with Happy. And Joe's Nan, Mrs Buxton, is clapping and swaying her head.

We are each handed an envelope and the trophy, a silver cup that Femi holds. Gary finishes by saying, 'Congratulations.'

'This feels just as good as winning the football tournament,' I say.

'Who is going to take the silver cup home?' asks Femi.

'I'm not bothered,' says Terry.

'I've already got one I won at judo,' says Sebastian.

'What about you, Joe?' I ask

'Oh, you have it, Tópé. I'm just glad you called me and let me be a part of the group, because it was such good fun,' says Joe.

'Are you really, really sure, Joe?' I ask.

'Yeah, I am, Tópé,' Joe says and he looks at me and smiles.

Joe's Nan comes to collect him to take him home, and Uncle and Aunty say they will take the rest of us home.

Joe turns around and calls back before he disappears, 'Don't forget about the boat.'

'Sure won't,' I smile.

As we drive home, I stare out of the window and realise that I'm now quite happy in England, even though I miss Nigeria. But there will always be a pain about not having my mum and dad any more. I can't wait to replace the two missing people in my boat with Joe and Uncle. I'm going to make the finest carvings ever.

Wendy Hue